AMAZING ANIMALS
OF THE WORLD ②

Volume 10

Tortoise, Gopher — Zebu

GROLIER

First published 2005 by Grolier, an imprint of Scholastic Library Publishing

For information address the publisher: Grolier, Scholastic Library Publishing
90 Old Sherman Turnpike
Danbury, CT 06816

Set ISBN: 0-7172-6112-3; Volume ISBN: 0-7172-6122-0

Printed and bound in the U.S.A.

Library of Congress Cataloging-in-Publications Data:
Amazing animals of the world 2.
p.cm.
Includes indexes.
Contents: v. 1. Adder—Buffalo, Water -- v. 2. Bunting, Corn—Cricket, Bush -- v. 3. Cricket, European Mole—Frog, Agile -- v. 4. Frog, Burrowing Tree—Guenon, Moustached -- v. 5. Gull, Great Black-backed—Loach, Stone -- v. 6. Locust, Migratory—Newt, Crested -- v. 7. Nuthatch, Eurasian—Razor, Pod -- v. 8. Reedbuck, Mountain—Snake, Tentacled -- v. 9. Snakefly—Toad, Surinam -- v. 10. Tortoise, Gopher—Zebu.
ISBN 0-7172-6112-3 (set : alk. paper) -- ISBN 0-7172-6113-1 (v. 1 : alk. paper) -- ISBN 0-7172-6114-X (v. 2 : alk. paper) -- ISBN 0-7172-6115-8 (v. 3 : alk. paper) -- ISBN 0-7172-6116-6 (v. 4 : alk. paper) -- ISBN 0-7172-6117-4 (v. 5 : alk. paper) -- ISBN 0-7172-6118-2 (v. 6 : alk. paper) -- ISBN 0-7172-6119-0 (v. 7 : alk. paper) -- ISBN 0-7172-6120-4 (v. 8 : alk. paper) -- ISBN 0-7172-6121-2 (v. 9 : alk. paper) -- ISBN 0-7172-6122-0 (v. 10 : alk.paper)
1. Animals--Juvenile literature. I. Title: Amazing animals of the world two. II. Grolier (Firm)
QL49.A455 2005
590--dc22

2005040351

About This Set

Amazing Animals of the World 2 brings you pictures of 400 fascinating creatures and important information about how and where they live.

Each page shows just one species—individual type—of animal. They all fall into seven main categories or groups of animals (classes and phylums scientifically) that appear on each page as an icon or picture—amphibians, arthropods, birds, fish, mammals, other invertebrates, and reptiles. Short explanations of what these group names mean, and other terms used commonly in the set, appear on page 4 in the Glossary.

Scientists use all kinds of groupings to help them sort out the thousands of types of animals that exist today and once wandered here (extinct species). Kingdoms, classes, phylums, genus, and species are among the key words here that are also explained in the Glossary (page 4).

Where animals live is important to know as well. Each of the species in this set lives in a particular place in the world, which you can see outlined on the map on each page. And in those locales the animals tend to favor a particular habitat—an environment the animal finds suitable for life, with food, shelter, and safety from predators that might eat it. There they also find ways to coexist with other animals in the area that might eat somewhat different food, use different homes, and so on. Each of the main habitats is named on the page and given an icon/picture to help you envision it. The habitat names are further

defined in the Glossary on page 4.

As well as being part of groups like species, animals fall into other categories that help us understand their lives or behavior. You will find these categories in the Glossary on page 4, where you will learn about carnivores, herbivores, and other types of animals.

And there is more information you might want about an animal—its size, diet, where it lives, and how it carries on its species—the way it creates its young. All these facts and more appear in the data boxes at the top of each page.

Finally, you should know that the set is arranged alphabetically by the most common name of the species. That puts most beetles, say, together in a group so you can compare them easily.

But some animals' names are not so common, and they don't appear near others like them. For instance, the chamois is a kind of goat or antelope. To find animals that are similar—or to locate any species—look in the index at the end of each book in the set (pages 45-48). It lists all animals by their various names (you will find the giant South American river turtle under turtle, giant South American river, and also under its other name— arrau). And you will find all birds, fish, and so on gathered under their broader groupings.

Similarly, smaller like groups appear in the set index as well—butterflies include swallowtails and blues, for example.

Table of Contents
Volume 10

Glossary

Amphibians—species usually born from eggs in water or wet places, which change (metamorphose) into a land animal. Frogs and salamanders are typical. They breathe through their skin mainly and have no scales.

Arctic and Antarctic—icy, cold, dry areas at the ends of the globe that lack trees but see small plants grown in thawed areas (tundra). Penguins and seals are common inhabitants.

Arthropods—animals with segmented bodies, hard outer skin, and jointed legs, such as spiders and crabs.

Birds—born from eggs, these creatures have wings and often can fly. Eagles, pigeons, and penguins are all birds, though penguins can't fly through the air.

Carnivores—they are animals that eat other animals. Many species do eat each other sometimes, and a few eat dead animals. Lions kill their prey and eat it, while vultures clean up dead bodies of animals.

Cities, Towns, and Farms—places where people live and have built or used the land and share it with many species. Sometimes these animals live in human homes or just nearby.

Class—part or division of a phylum.

Deserts—dry, often warm areas where animals often are more active on cooler nights or near water sources. Owls, scorpions, and jack rabbits are common in American deserts.

Endangered—some animals in this set are marked as endangered because it is possible they will become extinct soon.

Extinct—these species have died out altogether for whatever reason.

Family—part of an order.

Fish—water animals (aquatic) that typically are born from eggs and breathe through gills. Trout and eels are fish, though whales and dolphins are not (they are mammals).

Forests and Mountains—places where evergreen (coniferous) and leaf-shedding (deciduous) trees are common, or that rise in elevation to make cool, separate habitats. **Rainforests are different (see below).**

Fresh Water—lakes, rivers, and the like carry fresh water (unlike Oceans and Shores, where the water is salty). Fish and birds abound, as do insects, frogs, and mammals.

Genus—part of a family.

Grasslands—habitats with few trees and light rainfall. Grasslands often lie between forests and deserts, and they are home to birds, coyotes, antelope, and snakes, as well as many other kinds of animals.

Herbivores—these animals eat mainly plants. Typical are hoofed animals (ungulates) that are common on grasslands, such as antelope or deer. Domestic (nonwild) ones are cows and horses.

Hibernators—species that live in harsh areas with very cold winters slow down their functions then and sort of sleep through the hard times.

Kingdom—the largest division of species. Commonly there are understood to be five kingdoms: animals, plants, fungi, protists, and monerans.

Mammals—these creatures usually bear live young and feed them on milk from the mother. A few lay eggs (monotremes like the platypus) or nurse young in a pouch (marsupials like opossums and kangaroos).

Migrators—some species spend different seasons in different places, moving to where more food, warmth, or safety can be found. Birds often do this, sometimes over long distances, but others types of animals also move seasonally, including fish and mammals.

Oceans and Shores—seawater is salty, often deep, and huge. In it live many fish, invertebrates, and even some mammals, such as whales. On the shore birds and other creatures often gather.

Order—part of a class.

Other Invertebrates—animals that lack backbones or internal skeletons. Many, such as insects and shrimp, have hard outer coverings. Clams and worms are also invertebrates.

Phylum—part of a kingdom.

Rainforests—here huge trees grow among many other plants helped by the warm, wet environment. Thousands of species of animals also live in these rich habitats.

Reptiles—these species have scales, lungs to breathe, and lay eggs or give birth to live young. Dinosaurs are thought to have been reptiles, while today the class includes turtles, snakes, lizards, and crocodiles.

Scientific name—the genus and species name of a creature in Latin. For instance, Canis lupus is the wolf. Scientific names avoid the confusion possible with common names in any one language or across languages.

Species—a group of the same type of living thing. Part of an order.

Subspecies—a variant but quite similar part of a species.

Territorial—many animals mark out and defend a patch of ground as their home area. Birds and mammals may call quite small or quite large spots their territories.

Vertebrates—animals with backbones and skeletons under their skins

Gopher Tortoise
Gopherus polyphemus

Length: 9¼ to 14½ inches
Diet: mainly grasses and leaves
Number of Eggs: 2 to 7

Home: southeastern United States
Order: Turtles and tortoises
Family: Tortoises

 Grasslands

 Reptiles

© ZIGMUND LESZCZYNSKI / ANIMALS ANIMALS / EARTH SCENES

The gopher tortoise is a world-class digger—one of the longest burrows ever found was a straight, unbranched, nearly 50-foot-long tunnel excavated by this amazing creature. A typical burrow ends with a sleeping chamber where the air is cool and moist, unaltered by the outside weather. While the gopher tortoise rests inside its inner chamber, other animals may move into the adjoining tunnel.

The gopher tortoise emerges from its tunnel on cool, partly cloudy days. Typically it stops to rest at the entrance, soaking up warmth from the dim sunlight. Once its body is warm, the tortoise crawls out in search of food. Gopher tortoises live in sandy areas between grasslands and forests. They avoid low-lying areas, where water might flood their burrows. Unlike aquatic tortoises, which have webbed feet, the gopher tortoise does not swim. Its stumpy legs are flattened like shovels for digging.

Gopher tortoises mate in spring. The female may nest two or three times between late April and mid-July. She deposits each clutch of brittle, round eggs in a 5-inch-deep hole, often near the entrance to her burrow. In August and September, the baby tortoises hatch. They may spend a short time in their mother's burrow before digging their own. Unfortunately, this species is threatened with extinction in Alabama, Mississippi, and Louisiana. In these states, it is now illegal to disturb the species or keep it as a pet.

Spur-tailed Mediterranean Tortoise
Testudo hermanni

Length of the Shell: 4 to 10 inches

Diet: leaves, fruits, and other plant matter; also small invertebrates

Method of Reproduction: egg layer

Home: southern Europe

Order: Turtles and tortoises

Family: Tortoises

 Grasslands

 Reptiles

Many animals are named for a distinctive physical feature. As you might imagine, the spur-tailed Mediterranean tortoise sports a spur at the tip of its tail. It also has a thick, hard shell that is yellow with black markings. When the tortoise is attacked or senses danger, it simply pulls its head and legs completely inside the shell. The shell serves as a safe fortress.

Spur-tailed Mediterranean tortoises prefer dry habitats. They are common on rocky, grass-covered hillsides, farmlands, and backyard gardens. This creature is most active in the morning and late afternoon, and wisely spends the hottest part of the day at rest in the shade of a bush or low-growing tree. Spur-tailed Mediterranean tortoises love to eat plant matter, earthworms, snails, and other small invertebrates—all things that are abundant in their grassy habitats. Like all turtles and tortoises, spur-tails use the sharp edges of their jaws to chop food. They do not have teeth, so they cannot eat tough foods. And because they move very slowly, they seldom catch fast-moving animals.

These tortoises court and mate in spring. The female lays about 12 eggs in early summer, buries them in the ground, and then abandons them. At birth a spur-tailed Mediterranean tortoise is only about 2 inches long. Its shell is soft, and until the shell hardens, the baby tortoise is easy prey for birds and other hungry animals.

Tortoiseshell
Nymphalis sp.

Wingspan: up to 3 inches
Method of Reproduction: egg
  layer
Home: North and South
  America, Europe, Asia, and
  Africa

Diet: leaves (larva); tree sap
  and nectar (adult)
Order: Butterflies and moths
Family: Brush-footed
  butterflies

 Cities, Towns,
and Farms

 Arthropods

© ROBERT PICKETT / CORBIS

Three species of tortoiseshell occur in North America, and another three in Europe and Asia. These medium-size butterflies are named for the black, orange, and yellow markings on the undersides of their wings, which resemble markings on some tortoises. The wings are edged with many rounded notches. Some tortoiseshells look like dead leaves when their wings are folded—this disguise is a good example of nature's camouflage.

Tortoiseshells hibernate over the winter, hidden under bark or in small crevices. When they awaken in spring, they lay their barrel-shaped eggs on the twigs of trees on which their caterpillars will feed. In Europe the caterpillars once did serious damage to elm, poplar, and fruit trees. Today, however, the tortoiseshells are much rarer and so do little harm. In North America, these butterflies have never been numerous.

Most American tortoiseshells live in Canada and northern regions of the United States or in cool mountain regions. The small blackish-brown Milbert's tortoiseshell, *N. milberti*, lives along the East Coast and in the Rocky Mountains. The California tortoiseshell is brownish yellow with purple spots. The orange-brown Compton tortoiseshell, *N. vau-album*, is common throughout North America and parts of Europe.

Keel-billed Toucan
Ramphastos sulfuratus

Length: about 15 inches
Weight: about 12 ounces
Number of Eggs: 2 to 4
Home: Mexico south to Colombia and Venezuela

Diet: mainly fruits and insects
Order: Woodpeckers, toucans, and honeyguides
Family: Toucans

  Rainforests

Birds

© STEVE KAUFMAN / CORBIS

A gigantic bill with brilliant colors differentiates the toucan from other birds in the rainforest. The keel-billed toucan is named for the ridge that runs along the top edge of its curved upper beak. The ridge reminded early naturalists of a ship's keel, which is the projection that runs down the center of a boat's bottom.

Keel-billed toucans live in lowland jungles, where they feed high in the treetops. Their favorite foods include ripe berries and juicy, fat insects. Occasionally they also steal eggs and nestlings of smaller birds. The toucan picks up food with the tip of its beak and then tosses its head back, flipping the morsel into the rear of its mouth.

The toucan's beak is surprisingly light and strong. It is a hollow structure, reinforced on the inside by a honeycomb of thin, bony material. Biologists speculate that the bird's huge, colorful beak enables it to see and recognize other toucans in the shadowy jungle. Because toucans are territorial, a showy bill could also serve to warn away competitors.

These birds make their home in natural tree holes and large, abandoned woodpecker nests. Sometimes they must bend their long tail over their back to fit into the nest's entrance. Both parents care for the eggs and chicks.

Treehopper
Ceresa sp.

Length: about ½ inch
Method of Reproduction: egg layer
Home: North America and Europe

Diet: tree sap
Order: Aphids, scale insects, and their relatives
Family: Treehoppers

 Cities, Towns, and Farms

 Arthropods

© PATRICK GRACE / PHOTO RESEARCHERS

Treehoppers have always been common in North America and were inadvertently introduced into Europe during World War II. These dainty insects are known for the relatively large, hoodlike covering that extends over their head and upper body. This broad hood, called a "pronotum," can take on strange and peculiar shapes. Depending on the species of treehopper, the pronotum may look like a thorn, a hump, or a spine. In general, treehoppers resemble tiny leaves in both color and shape, so they are well camouflaged from their main enemies— birds and larger insects.

Several treehopper species are serious pests in fruit orchards. Most of the damage is done by the female when she lays her eggs in summer and fall. She deposits the eggs in slits that she cuts in the tender bark of twigs. The portion of the twig beyond the slits usually dies. The eggs lie dormant over the winter. They hatch in spring, and the larvae drop to the ground and feed on various plants.

The adult treehopper also causes damage when it feeds. Its mouthparts are shaped like a sharp beak. The insect uses its beak to pierce tree stems and draw sap. Some species of treehopper live in small groups that are tended by ants. The ants collect a sweet honeydew produced by the treehopper. In turn the ants protect the treehoppers from predatory insects and spiders.

Oak Treehopper
Platycotis sp.

Length: up to ½ inch
Method of Reproduction: egg layer
Home: tropical regions worldwide

Diet: sap
Order: Aphids, scale insects, and their relatives
Family: Treehoppers

 Rainforests

 Arthropods

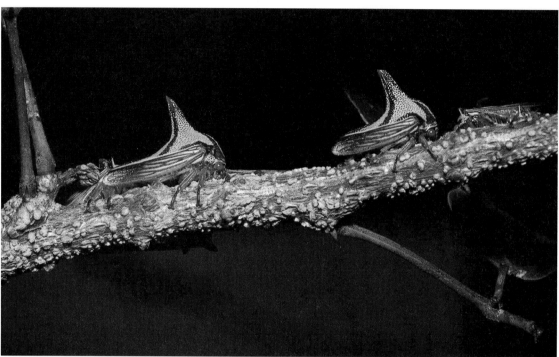

From its name, you might guess that this is an insect that hops on oak trees. But oak treehoppers are not found in temperate oak forests. They live in jungles. The insect is named for the strange growth on its back. The hump reminded early European naturalists of the bumps seen on oak trees.

The oak treehopper's hump (called a "prothorax") is quite ordinary compared to those of some treehoppers. There are more than 2,500 species of treehopper in the world, and most of them have some type of weirdly shaped prothorax. Some are shaped like thorns; others are inflated, pressed flat, stretched tall, or arched backward. The oak treehopper's prothorax looks as if it had been hammered like decorative copper.

What is the purpose of this hump? Some scientists believe that it is a form of camouflage that helps the treehopper look like a thorn or twig. Others argue that the unusual shape is just as likely to draw attention as it is to act as camouflage. Perhaps, like a peacock's feathers, the hump helps the insect attract a mate.

Despite its awkward-looking shape, the treehopper can run, jump, and fly quite well. Like other treehoppers, this species feeds largely on sap. Ants often gather herds of immature treehoppers and milk them for their sweet honeydew.

Redtooth Triggerfish
Odonus niger

Length: up to 2 feet
Diet: plankton, sponges, and other small invertebrates
Method of Reproduction: egg layer

Home: Indian and southern Pacific oceans
Order: Puffers
Family: Triggerfishes and filefishes

 Oceans and Shores

 Fish

© ALLAN POWER / BRUCE COLEMAN INC.

The redtooth triggerfish lives on the wave-swept, seaward side of coral reefs in the Indo-Pacific seas. Some have a black body, and others are blue. But all have distinctive red teeth.

The triggerfish's "trigger" is formed by three special spines on its back, which snap up when the fish is alarmed. The erect spines are a good defense against being eaten, because they make the triggerfish an unwieldy mouthful. Often a frightened triggerfish will dash into a crevice, headfirst, and then erect its spines. The sharp trigger wedges the fish in place so that it's nearly impossible to remove.

A mature male redtooth triggerfish is noticeably larger than the female. He stakes out and defends a wide territory that overlaps with the smaller territories of up to 10 females. Any smaller males that wander near are aggressively chased away.

When it's time to spawn, neighboring females gather together. In this way the male can defend his entire "harem" as they lay their eggs. Under his watchful eye, the females dig small pits in the sand, deposit their eggs, and guard them. The eggs hatch in just 12 to 14 hours, usually the night after they are laid. During this short incubation period, the females become brave and fierce. In defending their eggs, they will rush into the face of any intruder, even a human diver.

Undulate Triggerfish
Balistapus undulatus

Length: up to 9 inches
Diet: mollusks, crustaceans, corals, and fish
Method of Reproduction: egg layer

Home: Red Sea, Indian Ocean, and western Pacific Ocean
Order: Puffers
Family: Triggerfishes and filefishes

 Oceans and Shores

 Fish

© SECRET SEA VISIONS / PETER ARNOLD, INC.

When the triggerfish is frightened or attacked, it quickly swims into a hole in nearby rocks or coral and positions itself so it is facing the opening. Any animal that tries to attack the triggerfish faces a formidable mouth, which has powerful jaws and is lined with rows of sharp teeth.

To add to its defenses, the undulate triggerfish uses the spines on its dorsal, or rear, fin. The front spine is large and thick, while the second and third are smaller. When the triggerfish is backed up in a hole for defense, it can raise its spines to secure its position. The "trigger" is the third spine. When this spine bends backward, it releases the big first spine and locks the fish in its safe spot.

The undulate triggerfish lives at shallow depths in the warm, tropical Red Sea, Indian Ocean, and the western Pacific Ocean. It swims by rippling, or undulating, its dorsal fins—not by moving its tail in side-to-side motions as do most other fish

This is certainly one of the most beautifully colored fish in the world. Another common name for the undulate triggerfish is the yellow-striped emerald triggerfish. Some people add color to their aquariums with triggerfish. However, only very young undulate triggerfish are suitable for home aquariums, because the adults are too big and aggressive.

Turbot
Scophtalmus maximus

Length: up to 39 inches; typically about 15 inches
Weight: up to 26 pounds
Diet: fish
Number of Eggs: 5 million to 15 million

Home: Mediterranean Sea and northeastern Atlantic Ocean
Order: Flatfishes
Family: Turbots and their relatives

 Oceans and Shores

 Fish

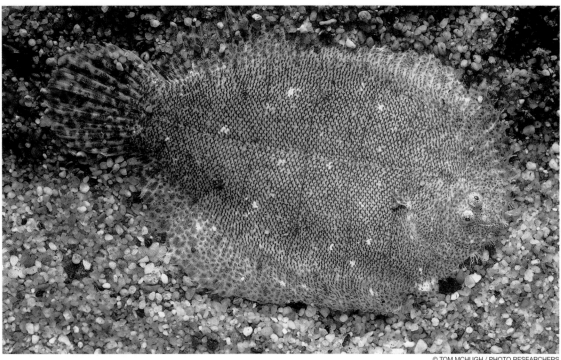

© TOM MCHUGH / PHOTO RESEARCHERS

As a newborn larva, the turbot looks and swims like most other fish. But when the larva is several days old, amazing physical changes begin to take place. The eye on the right side of its head moves to the left side, next to the other eye. Its dorsal fin extends onto the head. The two pectoral fins, which originally were of equal size, become unequal in size and shape. Soon after these changes occur, the little fish moves to the bottom of the ocean. There it settles with the eyeless side of its body resting on the ocean floor. It will spend most of its life in this position. Occasionally it will move, swimming sluggishly from side to side.

Turbot live at depths of about 60 to 230 feet. Young turbot eat shrimp and other crustaceans. As they grow bigger, they begin to catch sand eels, whiting, and other fish. Turbot mature slowly, but can grow to a very large size. However, because people enjoy eating turbot, these fish seldom get a chance to reach lengths of more than 20 inches. Most are caught by fishermen while the fish are still quite small. Also, many turbot are caught before they have reproduced. As a result, these fish are not as plentiful as they once were.

If given a chance to reproduce, the female lays millions of tiny eggs, which float on the ocean's surface. The eggs quickly hatch into larvae. Most of the eggs and larvae are eaten by predators or killed by poor environmental conditions.

Giant South American River Turtle (Arrau)
Podocnemis expansa

Length of the Carapace (Shell): up to 3½ feet
Diet: fruits, flowers, roots, and the soft parts of water plants
Method of Reproduction: egg layer

Home: northern South America and Trinidad
Order: Turtles and tortoises
Family: Hidden-necked turtles

 Fresh Water

 Reptiles

© MICHEL ROGGO / PETER ARNOLD, INC.

Endangered
Animals

The arrau, or giant South American river turtle, is one of the world's largest freshwater turtles. It lives in the Amazon River and its tributaries, and in the coastal rivers of Guyana and Venezuela. Occasionally floods wash the turtles into the ocean and to the island of Trinidad.

The arrau's large, flattened shell, or carapace, is oval and olive, gray, or brown. The carapace of a young arrau is marked with dark spots and a cream-colored border. Adults are recognized by the yellow spots on their chin and head. Arrau turtles have two shin barbels, or whiskers, with which they locate food in cloudy rivers. They also grow two or three large, strong scales on the back edge of each hind foot. The scales are useful shovels for digging up tasty roots and vegetation from the mud. At the beginning of the dry season, adults gather along sandy beaches, then enter the water to mate. For the next several weeks, the females bask in the sun onshore to speed the development of their eggs. They then dig deep nests in the sand and lay their eggs at night.

The arrau has long been hunted for its edible eggs, meat, and oil. Sadly, overhunting has brought the species dangerously close to extinction. Its numbers have also been reduced by the destruction of its rainforest habitat. Fortunately, arrau turtles are still abundant in a few small protected areas.

Helmeted Turtle
Pelomedusa subrufa

Length: 8 to 12½ inches
Diet: plants, frogs, small birds, insects, and crustaceans
Number of Eggs: 10 to 40

Home: Africa south of the Sahara
Order: Turtles and tortoises
Family: Hidden-necked turtles

 Fresh Water

Reptiles

The helmeted turtle is named for the shape and color of its carapace, or shell. Olive or brown in color, the carapace resembles a flattened military helmet. Like all cold-blooded animals, this turtle needs the heat of the sun to warm its body into action. But while other turtles move sluggishly, this African species travels quickly and fights fiercely.

After a strong rain, this turtle sets out in search of ponds and puddles. An aggressive hunter, it chases after large frogs and fish. It also catches small birds when they stop at the water's edge for a drink. Like most turtles, this species also eats lots of soft, aquatic plants.

After mating, females dig flask-shaped burrows in which they lay their soft eggs. About three months later, the young crack through their eggs. But as long as the weather and the ground remain dry, the hatchlings stay quietly buried. They emerge only when rain softens the soil.

An encounter with a helmeted turtle can be unpleasant. The creature is quarrelsome by nature, has a nasty bite, and can produce a foul odor. The turtle's best defense is to discourage its enemies because it has a difficult time withdrawing into its shell for protection. A helmeted turtle cannot retract its neck, but can only tuck it sideways under the lip of its shell.

Spotted Turtle
Clemmys guttata

Length: 3½ to 5 inches
Diet: green plants
Number of Eggs: up to 8
Home: eastern United States

Order: Turtles and tortoises
Family: Box turtles and water turtles

  Fresh Water

Reptiles

© JACK DERMID / BRUCE COLEMAN INC.

The spotted turtle is a particularly attractive species. Its rich black shell, or carapace, is splashed with bright yellow dots, which also decorate the turtle's head and legs. If you gently overturn a spotted turtle, you will see that its underside, called a plastron, is creamy yellow with a border of black splotches. You can easily tell a male from a female spotted turtle: The males all have brown eyes, while the female's are a dramatic orange. Their chins are different colors as well: The male's is tan, and the female's is yellow.

On cool spring days, the spotted turtle spends a lot of time basking in the sun. As the days grow hotter, this turtle disappears into the shade of tall grass and weeds. It prefers to live in marshy meadows and wet or boggy forests.

During late spring, spotted turtles mate. The fertilized female holds her eggs inside her body until June. She then digs a shallow hole in the shape of a flask and deposits about half a dozen soft-shelled eggs.

In the southern part of their range, spotted turtle babies dig out of their nest in late August and September. But in the North, the newborns remain inside their underground nest until the spring. They need very little air to survive. As adults, they will be able to stay on the bottom of a stream for hours, even days, without coming up for air. Hibernating spotted turtles may even sleep an entire winter underwater.

Unicornfish
Naso unicornis

Length: up to 2 feet
Width: under 3 inches
Diet: algae
Method of Reproduction: egg layer

Home: Indian and Pacific oceans
Order: Perchlike fishes
Family: Surgeonfishes

 Oceans and Shores

 Fish

© JEFF ROTMAN / PHOTO RESEARCHERS

The unicornfish belongs to a family of fish called surgeonfish. Their name comes from their fantastic, lancelike spines, which reminded early biologists of the sharp instruments a surgeon might use. Different surgeonfish wear their spikes in various parts of their body. As you might guess from the name unicornfish, this species's prong is between its eyes and can grow as long as 3 inches. The function of the horn remains a mystery. In fact, a horn would seem to be a handicap, getting in the way when the unicornfish browses for algae in coral reefs.

In addition to its unique horn, the unicornfish has two small, razor-sharp spines on each side of its tail. Though tiny, these tail spines are formidable weapons. The unicornfish can inflict slash wounds by lashing its spike tail from side to side.

The young unicornfish lacks spines. It does have a small bump on its nose, from which its horn will grow. Young unicornfish are also much scalier and flatter than adults. Young fish that look totally different from their parents are said to be "acronurus," or larval—in the same way as a caterpillar is a larval butterfly.

Like other surgeonfish of the Indo-Pacific oceans, the unicornfish is quite tasty. It is caught and sold commercially. You don't have to worry about its poisonous tail spikes—they are cut off before the fish is sold.

Slate-pencil Urchin
Eucidaris tribuloides

Width of the Body: about 2½ inches

Height: about 1¼ inches

Diet: mainly algae and dead animal matter

Method of Reproduction: egg layer

Home: western Atlantic Ocean from South Carolina to Brazil; also off the coast of Central Africa

Order: Primitive sea urchins

Family: Cidarid sea urchins

  Oceans and Shores

Other Invertebrates

© BRANDON D. COLE / CORBIS

The slate-pencil urchin is named for the shape and size of its long, thick spines. The surface of these large spines is often encrusted with barnacles, sponges, and other small marine creatures. The spines grow in attractive patterns on the urchin's globe-shaped body, or "test." Typically the urchin is reddish orange to brown, sometimes with spots and stripes.

This urchin slowly crawls over coral reefs and rocks, using its tiny tube feet and movable spines to get from one place to another. It usually lives in shallow water, often near the low-tide line. Like many species of sea urchin, this one feeds on dead fish and other animal matter that sinks to the ocean floor. It also scrapes algae off rocks and coral. Its central mouth—with five sharp teeth—is at the bottom of its body.

Like most urchins, this species has males and females, and reproduces by releasing eggs and sperm into the water. The swimming larvae that hatch look like tiny insects. They swim by moving their whirring hairs. Once the larvae grow large enough to settle on the seafloor, they mature into round, hard-bodied adults.

The slate-pencil urchin often sheds its large, blunt spines, which then wash onto the beaches in Bermuda, the Bahamas, and the West Indies. Local people string them together to make wind chimes that make a lovely sound.

Gaboon Viper
Bitis gabonica

Length: average 3 to 4 feet
Diet: small mammals and
　　ground birds
Number of Young: usually 24

Home: Africa
Order: Lizards and snakes
Family: Vipers and pit vipers

 Rainforests

 Reptiles

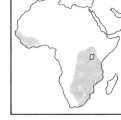

© JOE MCDONALD / CORBIS

The gaboon is Africa's largest viper and one of the most beautiful. Females can grow to a length of 7 feet. The snake's skin is decorated in a patchwork of pastel colors, including various shades of purple, yellow, black, and brown. In the dappled sunlight that reaches the jungle floor, the gaboon's soft coloring is perfect camouflage. Completing the disguise, this viper's large head is shaped like a fallen leaf. There is even a dark stripe across the top of the head that looks like the midrib on a real leaf. So camouflaged, the gaboon viper lies in ambush, waiting for its prey. It must rely on the element of surprise to kill, because it is heavy and slow.

Gaboon vipers are not picky eaters. They attack everything from frogs to small antelope. The gaboon bites deeply, sinking its 2-inch-long fangs into its victim's flesh. Its venom kills small animals almost instantly. Larger animals, including humans, are also affected by the venom. A person bitten by a large gaboon viper is likely to die unless a medical antidote is administered immediately.

Like many snakes, gaboon vipers give birth to live young. When they emerge from their mother's body, the newborn are 10 to 12 inches long. Although a typical litter consists of 24 snakelings, a large female gaboon may produce as many as 60 babies at one birth.

Russell's Viper (Daboia)
Vipera russelli

Length: 3 to 5½ feet
Home: Pakistan, India, Sri Lanka, southern China, Taiwan, Indochina, and Indonesia

Diet: mainly small rodents
Number of Young: 12 to 60
Order: Lizards and snakes
Family: Vipers and pit vipers

 Forests and Mountains

 Reptiles

© MICHAEL & PATRICIA FOGDEN / CORBIS

Russell's viper, which the people of India call the daboia, is a fat, heavy snake that can strike with tremendous power and speed. Its Indian name means "the lurker"—this dangerously poisonous snake spends the day hiding, coiled under stones or bushes. Unfortunately, the daboia's spotted brown body is so well camouflaged that it's easy to accidentally step on.

As a rule the daboia is too lazy to bother humans. But when disturbed, it hisses loudly and angrily, and then attacks with great force. The daboia's venom is a dangerous mix of chemicals that destroys its victim's blood. Without medical treatment the bite often proves deadly. Daboias often enter farms and brushlands near villages. As a result, they are a leading cause of poisonous snakebites in Southeast Asia. Adding to the problem is the tremendous speed at which daboias populate. A mature female gives birth to several dozen live young each year!

This viper also lives in mountain meadows and along the shrubby edges of wooded forests. As the sun sets, the snake emerges from its daytime hiding place to hunt through the night. Although its venom is toxic enough to kill large animals, the daboia feeds mainly on mice, gophers, and rats. This snake usually sneaks up quietly to ambush its dinner. Given their small size, prey animals die very quickly from the venom.

White-eyed Vireo
Vireo griseus

Length: 4½ to 5½ inches
Wingspan: 7½ to 8½ inches
Weight: ½ ounce or less
Diet: mainly insects and spiders; also berries and grapes

Number of Eggs: 3 to 5
Home: North America and Central America
Order: Perching birds
Family: Vireos

 Grasslands

 Birds

© F. J. ALSOP III / BRUCE COLEMAN INC.

The loud songs of white-eyed vireos often include notes that resemble human words. People in the southern United States think they hear the vireos saying, "Quick, take me to the railroad, quick!" People in Bermuda hear "gingerbeer, quick!" But the most common call seems to be "chick-a-per-wheeoo-chick!" White-eyed vireos also imitate the songs and notes of other birds, including the song sparrow and the American robin.

White-eyed vireos are most common at the edges of woods, in hedgerows, in swampy thickets, and on hillsides covered with blackberry bushes. They spend most of the time on or near the ground, where they hunt for insects and spiders. Occasionally the birds dine on berries, grapes, and other small fruit.

White-eyed vireos migrate. They breed in the eastern United States. In fall, they fly south to spend the winter in the southern United States, Mexico, and Central America. In early spring, they return to their northern homes.

When the white-eyed vireos reach their breeding grounds, the males court the females by fluffing their feathers, spreading their tail, and singing. The nest, which hangs from a branch several feet above the ground, is shaped much like a sac or purse. The two parents take turns incubating the speckled white eggs.

Plains Viscacha
Lagostomus maximus

Length: 25 to 34 inches
Weight: 15 to 20 pounds
(male); 7 to 10 pounds
(female)
Diet: grasses, grains, and
roots

Number of Young: 1 to 4
Home: Argentina and Bolivia
Order: Rodents
Family: Chinchillas and
viscachas

 Grasslands

 Mammals

© LEONARD LEE RUE III / PHOTO RESEARCHERS

The plains viscacha is the largest member of the chinchilla family. Unlike its softly furred cousins, the viscacha is covered with bristly hair. Its large eyes and ears provide keen sight and hearing at night. The male is particularly heavy, about double the weight of the female.

Although its fur is not valuable to humans, the plains viscacha is hunted relentlessly because the people of the South American pampas consider the creature to be a serious pest. When viscachas occur in large numbers, they destroy valuable grazing land with their strong urine, and they eat grasses that farmers grow for their own animals. To make matters worse, horses often trip and are injured in burrows made by the viscachas. As a result, hunters have totally destroyed the species over much of its range.

Scientists fear that the creature may be threatened with extinction if the slaughter continues. The viscacha's large burrows may be a nuisance, but they are also fascinating. Up to 50 animals may live in a single underground colony. Typically the burrow is started by an adult male, which digs a few simple tunnels. Eventually other family members expand the underground colony with more entrances, tunnels, and chambers. Some of the largest viscacha burrows in use are more than 70 years old. Over the years, large mounds of dirt pile up at the entrance holes. Viscachas decorate these piles with rocks, bones, and shiny objects such as tinfoil, buttons, and even lost keys.

European Water Vole
Arvicola terrestris

Length of the Body: 5½ to 8 inches
Length of the Tail: 2½ to 4 inches
Weight: 2½ to 11½ ounces

Diet: leaves, stems, and roots
Number of Young: 1 to 11
Home: Eurasia
Order: Rodents
Family: Burrowing rodents

 Fresh Water

 Mammals

© TONY TILFORD / OSF / ANIMALS ANIMALS / EARTH SCENES

The European water vole is about the size of a rat—and just as troublesome. It burrows under the ground in irrigated orchards and chomps away at tree roots. Some European water voles prefer the roots of specific varieties of apple trees. Others do great damage in well-watered gardens and farms by eating the roots of crops. According to farmers, it is nearly impossible to get rid of this vole. Still they try. Some put out poison apples, and others try to dig up the animal's vast underground burrows.

European water voles eat day and night, pausing only to nap every two or three hours. In the fall and winter, they build several food-storage chambers inside their long burrows. If the vole lives in the woods, it fills its storage cellars with the roots of dandelions and couch grass.

Some European water voles live in ponds, where they perch on floating nests made of matted plants. When they are hungry, the pond voles dive from their little rafts into the water, where they feed on underwater plants. Water voles can swim up to 590 feet before having to come up for air.

The European water vole's American cousin, Richardson's water vole, is virtually identical in appearance. This American water vole lives along the edges of mountain streams and lakes in Washington, Montana, British Columbia, and Alberta.

American Black Vulture
Coragyps atratus

Length: about 2 feet
Wingspan: up to 5 feet
Weight: 4 to 5 pounds
Diet: carcasses and young birds and other small animals

Number of Eggs: usually 2
Home: North, Central, and South America
Order: Birds of prey
Family: New World vultures

 Grasslands

 Birds

© JOE MCDONALD / CORBIS

The American black vulture frequents garbage dumps, picking through refuse and hunting rodents. Like all vultures, this species is attracted to the smell of rotting food and the flesh of dead animals. Black vultures have better eyesight than their vulture cousins. They use their superb vision as they soar high in the sky to spot small prey such as scurrying mice and young birds in their nests.

This species is also more social than most vultures. In winter, as many as 400 individuals may roost together in a stand of trees. It is likely that these large families share information on where to find carcasses and other food. During courtship, several males may chase a single female. They try to impress her by spiraling through the air above her head. After mating, the female lays her greenish eggs on a tree stump or in a thick mat of plants. Both parents tend the eggs and feed the young.

The black vulture is one of several large American birds of prey that can be difficult to tell apart. Seen from below, the black vulture is best recognized by its short, square tail and the white patches beneath its wings. Other American vultures and hawks have longer, narrower tails and darker underwings. At a carcass feast, black vultures are often seen alongside common turkey vultures. They can be distinguished by face color: the black vulture's is gray; the turkey vulture's is red.

Bearded Vulture
Gypaetus barbatus

Length: 4 feet
Wingspan: 8½ to 9 feet
Diet: mainly the flesh of dead animals
Number of Young: 1

Home: Europe, Africa, and Asia
Order: Birds of prey
Family: Old World vultures, buzzards, and their relatives

 Forests and Mountains

 Birds

© MICHEL GUNTHER / PETER ARNOLD, INC.

According to an old legend, Aeschylus, a famous playwright of ancient Greece, was killed by a bearded vulture. While in flight, the bird mistook Aeschylus's bald head for a stone and dropped a turtle on it. In the thousands of years since then, the bearded vulture still gets its favorite foods—marrow bones, turtles, and the flesh of dead animals—by simply swooping up the victim in its mouth and carrying it through the sky. Once the vulture spots a hard surface on the ground—bombs away! If the vulture is a good shot, the turtle's shell will crack, exposing the tasty inner flesh.

This vulture's "beard" is a collection of stiff black feathers that surround the creature's eyes and beak. Both sexes have beards, as well as broad wings and a long tail. Bearded vultures are powerful and graceful fliers, soaring to speeds of almost 80 miles per hour. They usually live in high mountain areas, but may be seen near farms, towns, and even garbage dumps, where they scavenge for insects and edible scraps.

Bearded vultures live in pairs. A couple stakes out a breeding territory, then makes a nest in a well-protected spot on a mountain cliff. There the female lays one or two eggs. She incubates the eggs, but may raise only one of the chicks, leaving the other to die. Both parents take turns feeding the surviving chick, which is ready to fly when it is about 16 weeks old.

King Vulture
Sarcoramphus papa

Length: about 31 inches
Number of Eggs: 1 or 2
Home: Central America and South America

Diet: dead animals
Order: Birds of prey
Family: New World vultures

 Rainforests

 Birds

© MICHAEL SEWELL / PETER ARNOLD, INC.

As its name implies, the king vulture rules whenever different species of vultures gather at a carcass. It is a bold, aggressive bird that takes what it wants and leaves the leftovers for more timid birds and animals. King vultures also have a reputation, possibly undeserved, for killing live animals. Although the vulture's long, hooked claws look fearsome, they are made for perching, not for attacking.

Like all vultures, this species has a featherless head and neck. This allows the bird to dive into messy carcasses headfirst, without soiling any feathers. The king vulture's bald head is marked with bright colors and weird flaps of skin. The male and female look quite similar. Young king vultures, however, are pure black. When they are nearly two years old, the young vultures develop a colorful face and white shoulders. This signals their readiness to mate.

Some king vultures hunt over grasslands, where dead animals are easy to spot from the air. But many king vultures live in tropical rainforests. In the jungle a bird cannot easily see through the thick and tangled plants to find a carcass on the ground. To adapt to jungle life, the king vulture has evolved a very sensitive sense of smell. It can sniff out rotting meat from a great distance. King vultures also use their nose to find fish that have washed ashore on riverbanks.

Lappet-faced Vulture
Torgos tracheliotus

Length: 39 to 45 inches
Weight: about 16 pounds
Diet: carcasses
Number of Eggs: 1

Home: Africa
Order: Birds of prey
Family: Hawks and their relatives

 Grasslands

 Birds

© ANUP SHAH / NATURE PICTURE LIBRARY

The gruesome-looking features of the lappet-faced vulture are perfect for its lifestyle. Its strong, hooked bill rips apart the flesh of large, dead animals. A bald head and naked face save the vulture from having to clean the blood and gore from its feathers after each messy meal. This vulture was named "lappet-faced" for the folds of bright skin on its head and face. They reminded early European naturalists of the flaps, or "lappets," sewn onto hats of their day.

Like vultures around the world, this species soars high in the sky. Using broad and powerful wings, vultures can glide effortlessly for hours. As they ride the wind currents, these birds continually scan the ground for freshly dead or dying animals.

Lappet-faced vultures mature slowly and have a long life expectancy. Only when they are several years old are these birds ready to mate. Their courtship is simple, with no showy displays. Once they mate, the male and female build a huge nest of sticks atop a tall tree or in the crevice of a cliff.

The lappet-faced vulture greatly resembles the turkey vulture of the southwestern United States. Both species have red, naked faces, downward-curving bills, and dark-brown feathers. However, they are not closely related. The vultures of the Old and New World evolved separately but similarly because they perform the same job in comparable habitats.

White Wagtail
Motacilla alba

Length: 7 inches
Number of Eggs: 5 or 6
Home: *Summer:* Europe, Asia, and northern Africa

Winter: Asia and Africa
Diet: insects
Order: Perching birds
Family: Pipits and wagtails

 Cities, Towns, and Farms

 Birds

Summer ☐ Winter ☐

© FRITS HOUTKAMP / FOTO NATURA / MINDEN PICTURES

True to its name, the wagtail constantly twitches its long tail up and down like a nervous cat. Just before launching itself into the air, the white wagtail races along the ground, its tail flapping as fast as its wings.

The white wagtail prefers to stay near water and often wades into marshes and shallow pools. Hundreds of white wagtails may roost together in reedbeds or adjoining trees. They often build their grassy, cup-shaped nests in natural cubbyholes along steep river embankments. Sometimes the birds nest in shallow depressions in the ground or in the crevices of houses or other buildings.

The white wagtail spends most of the day on the ground, taking to the air only to catch flying insects. It may even follow horses and cattle, snapping up the bugs that the grazing animals send into the air. White wagtails tend to twitter as they work. If alarmed, they warn their friends with a shrill "tchizzik!"

The handsome white wagtail, a very long and slender bird, can be recognized by its neat black-and-white suit. In winter, its species has two distinct races, or subspecies. The white wagtail lives in continental Europe and Asia, and sports a light gray back and rump during the summer. The British subspecies, also called the pied wagtail, is darker. Sometimes the two species flock together on their way to southern Africa and Asia for the winter.

Yellow Wagtail
Motacilla flava

Length: about 6½ inches
Number of Young: 5 or 6
Home: Alaska, the Yukon (Canada), Europe, Asia, and Africa

Diet: insects, worms, snails, slugs, and berries
Order: Perching birds
Family: Pipits and wagtails

 Grasslands

 Birds

© TONY HAMBLIN / FRANK LANE PICTURE AGENCY / CORBIS

Yellow wagtails love to run in large groups through the underbrush. The flock's graceful movements flush insects into the air. This allows the birds an easy opportunity to catch dinner. Small and slender, the wagtail can be recognized by its long tail, streamlined body, and narrow, pointed beak. True to its name, the wagtail continuously flips its tail up and down as it stands.

The yellow wagtail is best distinguished from others in its family by a bright yellow belly, greenish back, and black tail. Within the species, there are several distinct subspecies. Although each subspecies mates only with its own kind, they may flock together when it's time to migrate. Most yellow wagtails spend the winter in tropical Africa, where they live on the banks of rivers, lakes, and streams.

In spring, after the yellow wagtails return north, the males perform their courtship displays. Before breeding with his chosen mate, the male yellow wagtail flies some 60 to 90 feet over her head. He then glides downward on open wings, singing sweetly. On the ground the male puffs up his feathers, fans his tail, and vibrates his wings, as if he were shivering from the cold. After mating, the female builds a cup-shaped nest on the ground, usually hidden beneath bushes or weeds. She weaves the nest out of plant fibers and lines it with soft fur and hair. Her eggs hatch less than two weeks after they are laid.

Red-cheeked (Cordon-bleu) Waxbill
Uraeginthus bengalus

Length: about 5 inches
Weight: about ⅓ ounce
Diet: grass seeds and cereal crops

Number of Eggs: 4 or 5
Home: Africa
Order: Perching birds
Family: Weaver finches

 Grasslands

 Birds

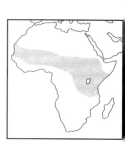

© JAMES URBACH / SUPERSTOCK

The male red-cheeked, or cordon-bleu, waxbill does justice to his colorful name. But the female and young have rather dull feathers. Red-cheeked cordon bleus are one of several African cordon-bleu finches. The males all have eye-catching blue breasts and tails. The bright tail feathers reminded European naturalists of the blue ribbons, or "cordon bleus," that aristocrats often pinned on their jackets. The Europeans brought many of these beautiful birds back with them as cage birds. Red-cheeked cordon bleus become quite tame and often breed in captivity. They are now popular pets around the world.

This species of cordon bleu is very common throughout the savannas of central Africa. The introduction of modern farming has helped extend the bird's range into new areas because cultivated fields provide plenty of tasty seeds. Like other finches, cordon bleus spend most of their time scavenging on the ground for fallen seeds and grain.

Unlike typical finches, the red-cheeked cordon bleu does not gather in large flocks. Instead, it prefers to live in pairs or small families. Each mated pair builds a globe-shaped nest with a small entrance hole on the side. This enclosed nest is woven out of long strands of dry grass and is typically found in a bush or a tree. The birds also weave their nests inside the thatched roofs common in African villages.

Cedar Waxwing
Bombycilla cedrorum

Length: 7 inches
Home: North and Central America, from Alaska to Panama

Diet: mainly berries and fruits
Number of Eggs: 3 to 5
Order: Perching birds
Family: Waxwings

Cities, Towns, and Farms

Birds

© WAYNE LANKINEN / BRUCE COLEMAN, INC.

Despite its elegant appearance, this songbird has a reputation for gluttony. A flock of cedar waxwings can quickly strip an entire tree or field of berries. These birds seem to greatly enjoy their feast as they trill and chatter with one another. Often cedar waxwings in a flock will pass berries back and forth to one another. To the delight of bird-watchers, cedar waxwings don't seem to mind close observers.

Waxwings get their name from the red, waxy droplets that form on their wingtips. Bird experts do not fully understand the function of this brightly colored wax that is seen only on mature waxwings that are at least three years old. The red mark may be an important sign of maturity. Scientists do know that older waxwings prefer to mate with each other, rather than with younger adults. Perhaps more mature waxwings make better parents.

Mated cedar waxwings build their nest high in coniferous trees such as cedars. Their nest is a woven cup of twigs and grass, lined with moss, hair, pine needles, and stringy roots. Their eggs are a pale bluish gray with black or brown spots. When their chicks hatch, the parents feed them insects. But within a few days, the nestlings can eat adult food—namely berries. Cedar waxwings also enjoy eating drops of sweet tree sap and certain plant blossoms.

Grenadier Weaver (Red Bishop)
Euplectes orix

Length: about 5 inches
Weight: about ½ ounce
Diet: seeds and grain
Number of Eggs: 3

Home: Africa
Order: Perching birds
Family: Weavers

 Grasslands

 Birds

© NIGEL J. DENNIS / PHOTO RESEARCHERS

When early European naturalists first saw this crimson-feathered bird, they thought of the red caps and robes worn by their high-ranking priests and bishops. And so the red bishop was named. Actually it is only the male bishop that earns the name. He turns into a fuzzy red-and-black ball each spring. The female red bishop is a dull brown, as is the male outside of breeding season.

Red bishops are abundant throughout the grasslands of Africa, especially near water. Each adult male competes with other males to establish a territory. Within it, he weaves several tall, oval-shaped nests among the sturdy grasses and reeds. His goal is to win three or four mates, one for each of his nests. He does so by soaring through the air while singing and showing off his bright red feathers. Once he attracts a female and mates in midair, the male leads her to the side entrance of one of his nests. She then lines the inside of the nest with soft materials and lays her eggs.

The female remains behind, incubating her eggs, while the male flies away to find another mate. When the chicks hatch in 11 to 14 days, the mother feeds them insects. Once they learn to fly, the young birds eat seeds and grain, as do their parents. In fact, red bishops eat so much grain that they can severely damage farm crops. Away from farmland, they are content to feed on grass seeds alone.

Wels

Silurus glanis

Length: up to 9¾ feet
Weight: up to 660 pounds
Method of Reproduction: egg layer

Diet: fish and small animals
Home: Europe and Asia
Order: Catfishes
Family: Sheatfishes

 Fresh Water

 Fish

© JEAN ROCHE / PETER ARNOLD, INC.

The wels is the largest catfish in the world, with a voracious appetite that matches its size. It is strictly a meat eater, and its wide, flattened mouth fits around very large prey. In the water the wels gobbles down other fish as well as frogs. Jumping above the surface, it can grab ahold of birds and small mammals that come to the water's edge.

Welses are most active at night and do much of their prowling along the bottom of the water. In Europe, they live in muddy lakes and large rivers with deep pools. During the day, they may rest under sunken trees or beneath overhanging riverbanks.

In spring, some welses make long migrations upriver to spawn in shallow water. The male constructs a mound of leaves, into which the female deposits her eggs. Her mate then guards the eggs. As soon as the eggs hatch, the exhausted adults float back downstream to deeper water, where they rest and overwinter. Meanwhile the hungry newborn gobble anything that fits into their mouth. The young catfish grow quickly, reaching a length of one foot in their first year.

Welses are very important commercial fish for the Europeans. The young fish are a delicious source of food. Larger welses are processed for fish meal and fertilizer. Their skin is made into leather and their eggs into caviar. Anglers are fond of this catfish because it takes any meat bait. Tussling with a large wels takes strength and skill.

Baird's Beaked Whale
Berardius bairdi

Length: 32 to 38 feet
Weight: up to 10 tons
Diet: squid, crabs, fish, and starfish
Number of Young: 1

Home: northern Pacific Ocean
Order: Whales, dolphins, and porpoises
Family: Beaked whales
Suborder: Toothed whales

 Oceans and Shores

Mammals

© RICHARD ELLIS / PHOTO RESEARCHERS

Sleek and fast, Baird's beaked whale is a deep-sea diver somewhat longer and more slender than a killer whale. No one has ever captured this animal, the largest of the beaked whales, alive. What we know about Baird's beaked whale comes from those killed by Japanese whalers. In the 1950s the Japanese killed more than 300 Baird's beaked whales each year. Today whalers do not find many, because their hunting has severely reduced the whale's population. Is Baird's beaked whale in danger of extinction? No one knows for sure.

This beaked whale is also called the "four-tooth whale," because of the two pairs of tusks jutting up from the male's lower jaw. Biologists believe that the whale may use its tusks to fight with other whales over territory and mates. As evidence, Baird's beaked whales have many long scars streaking their dark bodies. If the scars are battle wounds, they suggest that the whales bite deeply, but not so fiercely as to kill each other.

Beaked whales eat like vacuum cleaners, sucking in slippery squid and small crustaceans. They probably swallow their food whole, since they don't have enough teeth to do much chewing. While most beaked whales live a solitary life, Baird's are known to hunt in small schools, or pods. It is believed that males and females usually travel in separate groups.

Waved Whelk
Buccinum undatum

Length of the Shell: 2¾ to 3½ inches
Diet: marine worms, clams, and rotting meat
Home: North Atlantic Ocean

Method of Reproduction: egg layer
Order: Marine snails
Family: Whelks

 Oceans and Shores

 Other Invertebrates

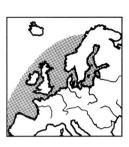

© ANDREW J. MARTINEZ / PHOTO RESEARCHERS

The waved whelk is found along the North Atlantic coast. Unlike many snail-like mollusks from our coasts, it cannot stay out of the water very long, even though its body is protected by a thick gray to yellowish shell.

The whelk moves on the bottom of the sea using its muscular foot, just like the snail. It moves slowly, going against the current and guided by its sense of smell. The whelk has a sort of tube called the syphon that it draws out to locate dead marine animals. Besides finding food, the syphon has a breathing function. Water that enters it brings oxygen to the snail, along with the smell of food. This snail is the great "cleaner" of the sea because it eats nothing but dead animals. The whelk uses its rough tongue, the radula, to take the food apart.

From midfall to the following spring, the female produces up to 500 egg capsules less than an inch wide. Each capsule can hold 2,000 eggs. One month later, only 1 egg out of 100 will hatch. Most of the other eggs will have fed embryos that developed first. The empty capsules are then washed onto beaches.

Even dead, the waved whelk is still helpful to some marine animals. Its empty shell is a favorite home for the hermit crab. It is also a good anchor for a sea anemone.

Marbled White
Melanargia galathea

Wingspan: 1½ to 2 inches
Diet: grasses (caterpillar)
Method of Reproduction: egg layer

Home: Europe and northern Asia
Order: Butterflies and moths
Family: Wood nymphs

 Grasslands

 Arthropods

© GEORGE MCCARTHY / CORBIS

The pretty marbled white is one of the most familiar butterflies in Europe. Throughout summer, it flutters over flowery grasslands, open meadows, and light woodlands. Although unremarkable in color, this butterfly is easily recognized by its slow, distinctive flight. The female tends to be larger and whiter than the male.

The female has an unusual way of laying her eggs. She sits on a tall blade of grass or flower stem with her wings open. Then she wriggles her body until a white, barrel-shaped egg appears at her rear end. Finally she zooms into the air as her egg drops to the ground.

When it hatches, the dark larva, or grub, hides on a blade of grass and hibernates through the winter. In spring the grub grows into a brown caterpillar covered with fine hair. At first the caterpillar keeps its head hidden near the ground. When it is larger, it wriggles inside a clump of grass, which serves as food and shelter. At the end of spring, the caterpillar spins a cocoon, usually in the dirt or under some leaves. Inside, it transforms itself into an adult butterfly. Today marbled whites are spreading into new areas where forests have been thinned or cut down. But they are slowly disappearing from regions where grazing animals have destroyed wild grasslands.

36

Pin-tailed Whydah
Vidua macroura

Length of the Body: about 5 inches
Length of the Tail of a Breeding Male: about 7½ inches
Weight: about ½ ounce

Diet: seeds and insects
Number of Eggs: 2 or 3
Home: central Africa
Order: Perching birds
Family: Weavers

 Grasslands

 Birds

© ROB DRUMMOND / LONELY PLANET IMAGES

The pin-tailed whydah, or "widow" bird, is named for the breeding dress of the adult male. During mating season, his feathers become glossy black (like a widow's dress in mourning), and he grows four very long tail streamers. In this bold plumage, the breeding male is quite conspicuous. To further draw attention to himself, he soars over his territory, singing loudly. Once the love-struck suitor attracts a female, he hovers directly over her head, displaying his showy tail feathers.

The female whydah is a parasitic bird that deposits her eggs in the nests of gray waxbills. In doing so, the whydah fools the waxbill into incubating her eggs and raising her chicks. Whydahs occasionally destroy the eggs of the bird whose nest they invade, but this is not always the case. Moreover, pin-tailed whydah chicks do not kill their foster mother's chicks, as do many other parasitic birds. Instead, they seem to get along well with their foster family and may stay with them for several months after leaving the nest.

Once mating season is over, male pin-tailed whydahs lose their long tail streamers and take on the drab coloring of the females. During the winter, these birds gather in large flocks that feed among the grasses of Africa's vast savanna. For the most part, the birds survive on small insects, which they scratch from the ground with both feet.

Maned Wolf
Chrysocyon brachyurus

Length of the Body: 3½ feet
Length of the Tail: 15 inches
Weight: up to 55 pounds
Diet: small animals, eggs, and plants

Number of Young: 1 to 5
Home: South America
Order: Carnivores
Family: Dogs

 Grasslands

 Mammals

© TOM BRAKEFIELD / CORBIS

The maned wolf was born to run. With its extremely long legs, the wolf can move swiftly through the tall grasses that cover its habitat. Its height also allows the wolf to see over the top of the grass in its South American habitat. Some people have described the maned wolf as a fox on stilts.

The maned wolf is named for the dark mane of hair on its neck. The wolf raises its mane when it feels threatened or wants to frighten away other animals. But this creature is usually shy and prefers to live alone. It stakes out a large territory of its own and marks the area with urine. Fiercely possessive of its territory, the wolf will threaten, and may even fight, any other maned wolf that crosses the urine path.

The maned wolf usually hunts at night, relying on its excellent senses of sight, hearing, and smell. Typically, it lies in wait for insects, lizards, agoutis, pacas, and other small animals. When prey comes near, the maned wolf leaps at the prey, grabs it in its mouth, and shakes the victim to death. When its usual prey is not available, the maned wolf adds bird eggs and plants to its diet. Sometimes the wolf will even store food for use at a later time. When in storing mode, the wolf digs a hole in the ground with its front paws, puts the food in the hole, and then uses it snout to cover the hole with soil. The wolf will return to this "pantry" when food is scarce in the wild.

38

Horsehair Worm
Gordius sp.

Length: up to 2½ feet
Diet: insect tissues (larva)
Number of Eggs: millions

Home: worldwide
Order: Gordoids
Family: Gordoids

  Fresh Water

Other Invertebrates

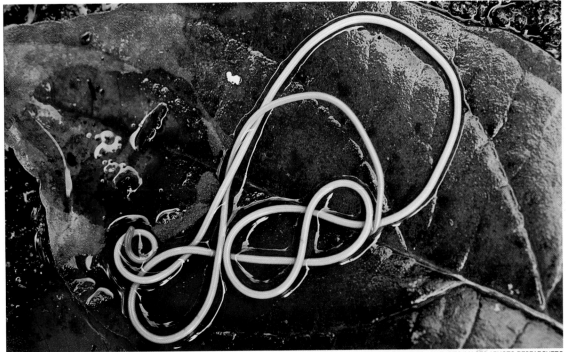

© DAVID SCHLESER / NATURE'S IMAGES / PHOTO RESEARCHERS

Horsehair worms are freshwater creatures named for their tough, hairlike body. English country folk used to call these worms "water calves" because they seemed to appear miraculously in water. Early scientists also questioned why they could find only adult horsehair worms. Where were their immature forms, or larvae? It was later discovered that horsehair worms develop inside the bodies of insects.

The horsehair worm's fascinating story begins when an adult female sheds a long string of eggs into the water. The larvae that hatch are less than ¹⁄₂₀th of an inch long. Each tiny larva has a pointy snout with three little spears and three rings of sharp

hooks. Like a pirate boarding a sailing ship, the horsehair larva hooks onto a passing water beetle larva. Then it bores inside its host, where it develops into an adult worm. If the pond in which it lives dries out, the larva will encase itself in a little capsule. The capsule is occasionally eaten by grasshoppers or carabid beetles, which also serve as hosts.

When fully grown, the worm returns to the water. Although it has eaten some of its host's body tissue, it does little harm. Somehow horsehair worms that live inside grasshoppers and land beetles prompt their hosts to seek water, where the worms can escape. The adult worm does not eat. It simply dies after laying its eggs.

Ice Cream Cone Worm
Pectinaria gouldii

Length: about 1½ inches
Width: about ¼ inch
Diet: plankton animals and dissolved animal matter
Method of Reproduction: egg layer

Home: East Coast of United States
Order: Sedentary polychaetes
Family: Pectinarid polychaete worms

 Oceans and Shores

Other Invertebrates

The ice cream cone worm is a skillful stonemason. It carefully gathers small grains of sand, one at a time, and sorts them according to size and shape. When it has a perfect set of sand grains, the worm cements them into a hard ring around its body. In this manner the worm encases itself inside a hard tube that is one grain of sand thick. The top end of the worm's tube is wider than the bottom, so the entire tube resembles a tiny ice cream cone. The tube is only slightly larger than the worm's body.

Ice cream cone worms live in estuaries, which form where rivers and streams empty into the sea. The water in an estuary is a mixture of fresh and salty water. Normally this worm and its tube remain buried—straight up and down—in the sandy mud at the bottom of an estuary. But after a storm, many beautiful tubes wash onto the beach. Inside the tube is the worm's soft creamy-pink body. Its head is flattened and has two pairs of long antennae. The worm breathes through two sets of bright red gills. It feeds by sifting tiny bits of food from the water using its cream-colored tentacles and feeding bristles.

The species *Pectinaria gouldii* is found only on the East Coast. On the West Coast are two cousins, the California ice cream cone worm, *P. californiensis*, and the coarse-grained ice cream worm, *Cistenides brevicoma*.

40

Peripatus Velvet Worm
Peripatus sp.

Length: up to 6 inches
Diet: mainly crickets, termites, and spiders
Method of Reproduction: egg layer

Home: Central and South America
Order: Velvet worms
Family: Peripatid velvet worms

  Rainforests

Other Invertebrates

© CLIFF B. FRITH / BRUCE COLEMAN INC.

Peripatus velvet worms live in the dark, damp corners of the American tropics. They crawl through the night on stumpy legs that bear small, sharp claws. Slowly and patiently, the peripatus searches for prey by sweeping its head and sensitive antennae from side to side. In this way, it can sense the presence of an insect an inch or so away.

Once it senses food, the peripatus touches its prey by stretching out its accordionlike antennae. If the worm decides that it has found something edible, it attacks. First it squirts a stream of glue from special slime glands around the mouth. The insect prey becomes tangled in the sticky threads and thrashes helplessly. If the insect is very active, the peripatus directs some extra glue around the victim's legs.

The peripatus velvet worm has a large mouth on the underside of its head. It is equipped with strong jaws that resemble sharp blades. When the worm bites, it injects a fluid that dissolves its victim's flesh into mush. Then the peripatus sucks up the softened tissue.

The velvet worm is covered with countless fingerlike bumps, which give the creature its velvety texture. Velvet worms are neither true worms nor arthropods (like centipedes and millipedes). But like earthworms, they have a long, soft body. And like a millipede, it has antennae and many legs.

Red Tube Worm
Serpula vermicularis

Length: up to 3 inches
Home: Pacific Ocean, northern Atlantic Ocean, Mediterranean Sea, English Channel, and North Sea

Diet: phytoplankton and zooplankton particles
Number of Eggs: 300 to 700
Order: Tube worms
Family: Calcerous tube worms

 Oceans and Shores

 Other Invertebrates

© GARY RETHERFORD / PHOTO RESEARCHERS

The red tube worm is not as flashy as its name might imply. Red is simply a highlight on its delicate tentacles. This sea creature is also known as the chalk tube worm; its external calcium skeleton looks much like a pink stick of chalk.

Keeping its soft body safe inside its hard skeleton, the tube worm extends it delicate tentacles in search of food. Bits of passing plankton cling to tiny hairs on the tentacles. With a constant brushing motion, the hairs sweep food into the worm's open mouth. The tentacles of the red tube worm are extremely sensitive to light. The mere shadow of a passing fish triggers a reflex that snaps the tender tentacles back into their protective tube. The tube worm has a red, trumpet-shaped appendage next to its feeding tentacles. When it withdraws its tentacles, the worm pulls this red trumpet over the opening of its tube—like a lid. But the lid is lined with many small teeth. Their prick is usually enough to discourage any predator from attacking the sealed-off worm.

Tiny red tube worms can be found glued to stones, rocks, and shells in the shallow waters around Western Europe and the East Coast of North America. Like the other members of its family, the red tube worm makes its tube from a calcium goo secreted from special glands in its body. The soft worm can move up and down within the tube by undulating in a way that creates a small wave that rolls down its back.

Superb Blue Wren
Malurus cyaneus

Length: 5½ inches
Diet: insects and their larvae
Number of Eggs: 3 or 4

Home: southeastern Australia
Order: Perching birds
Family: Wren warblers

Cities, Towns, and Farms

Birds

© MARTIN B. WITHERS / FRANK LANE PICTURE AGENCY / CORBIS

During the breeding season, the male superb blue wren becomes quite a colorful character. Striking bright blue feathers cover his head, upper back, and tail. When the breeding season ends, he sheds, or molts, these blue feathers and grows a new coat of mousy brown and white feathers that is similar to the coat of the female. But the male and female wrens are still easy to distinguish, because the male has a black bill, while the female has a reddish-brown one.

Because they are weak fliers, the superb blue wrens spend most of their time on the ground or on shrubs or fence posts. They find all of their food on or near the ground,

snapping up beetles and other tasty insects with their bill. The wren's lovely song can fill a spring or summer evening with music.

This bird is common only in the southeastern part of Australia. It tends to settle in dense shrubs that are near open areas, such as swamps, riverside thickets, orchards, gardens, and golf courses.

During the breeding season, the female builds a dome-shaped nest out of grasses, twigs, and small roots in a well-hidden thicket or clump of tall grass. She gathers feathers, plant fibers, and other soft materials to line the inside of the nest. A male and female wren usually raise two broods of babies each year.

Zebu
Bos indicus

Height at the Shoulder: 3 to 3½ feet
Weight: 1,000 to 2,200 pounds
Diet: mainly grasses
Number of Young: usually 1

Home: native to India; introduced elsewhere
Order: Even-toed hoofed mammals
Family: Bovines

 Cities, Towns, and Farms

 Mammals

© CHRIS HELLER / CORBIS

More than 6,000 years ago, people in Asia domesticated cattle now called zebus. In the many centuries since then, zebus have been extremely important to humans. People use zebus to carry heavy loads and to ride from place to place. They are strong creatures that thrive in hot weather and resist ticks and many diseases.

The zebu can be recognized by the hump of fatty tissue on its shoulders, a feature evident even in newborns. The creature also has long horns and a very large dewlap (a flap of skin that hangs between the front legs). Like other cattle, the zebu is a cud chewer, or ruminant. It only partly chews its food and swallows it. Later the zebu brings the cud (food) back into its mouth and chews it some more. It then swallows the food again and digests it.

Unlike modern-day cattle, the zebu does not represent a good source of meat and milk. People have, however, bred zebus with other kinds of domesticated cattle. This has created new kinds of cattle called dual-purpose breeds. One of these breeds is the Brahman, which produces good meat, is tick- and disease-resistant, and does well in hot climates.

Hindus consider zebus and other cattle to be sacred animals. Zebus are allowed to roam through the streets of India. Hindus use the animals for work, but they do not kill them.

Set Index